CW01463856

The Book of
Healing Words

with love
from

Denise Crabtree

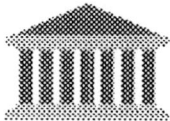

Stonecliffe Publishing
Welton - Lincolnshire - England

© Denise Crabtree 1995

ISBN 1 898086 03 6

This book is copyright under the Berne Convention. All rights are reserved. Apart from any fair dealing for the purpose of private study, research, criticism or review, as permitted under the Copyright Act, 1956, no part of this publication may be reproduced, stored in a retrieval system, or transmitted, in any form or by any means, electronic, electrical, chemical, mechanical, optical, photocopying, recording or otherwise, without the prior permission of the copyright owner. Enquiries should be addressed to the Publishers.

British Library Cataloguing-in-Publication Data
A catalogue record for this book is available
from the British Library

Computer typeset by

Stonecliffe Publishing,
P.O. Box 11, Welton, Lincolnshire, LN2 3HY
England.

Printed and bound in Great Britain by
Antony Rowe Ltd, Chippenham, Wiltshire

The Book of Healing Words

A Book of inspirational verse, capturing the thoughts and feelings that, at times, all of us experience. And through these poems comes peace, tranquillity and healing, which the reader may receive from the text.

✳ ✳ ✳ ✳ ✳

Dedication

✻ ✻ ✻ ✻

To my husband Steve and my parents
With love.

Acknowledgement

With thanks to my family and friends for their encouragement and support, without which these poems would not have been published.

Introduction

Dear Reader,

It is with much joy I share these poems with you. They have been written here at my home in the Brendon Hills in the Somerset village of Huish Champflower, where I have been fortunate enough to live all my life, surrounded by kind, warm hearted people and beautiful countryside.

I very much hope you enjoy 'The Book of Healing Words' and that it may inspire you, comfort you and bring you peace.

With best wishes.

Denise Crabtree
Huish Champflower
Somerset
March 1995

Although your life may be busy,
Take a little time to receive God's
Healing and Blessing.
Lift up a prayer, no matter how
small,
And His Light shall shine upon
you.

The Well Worn Path

"I am the way, the truth and the
light," that's what Jesus said.
Perhaps we might remember this as
along our paths we tread.

As to place our feet in the footsteps of
one that has gone before.
Makes the route far easier and much
less of a chore.

So if we all were to tread where Jesus
has gone before,
Placing our footsteps in His, we could
face more confidently, what life holds
in store.

So why not use that well worn path
which lies in front of you?
Walk where many have gone before,
in faith, in love, you'll be guided too.

For once you're walking along that
beautiful sacred pathway,
God touches you, guides and protects
you, in His own very special way.

✻ ✻ ✻ ✻

Through Life's Forest

I am passing through a forest that is
both shady and dark.
The trees tower above and all about
me, covered by a dark brown bark.

There is a black inky night sky.
With the odd star studding it's
darkness way up high.

But as I search my weary way through
life's wood.
I see far in the distance a clearing full
of light, which radiates only good.

As I head towards it, I might sometimes
stumble or fall.
But as I become closer, with every step
I take, its as if I'm answering a call.

For even though this clear uplifting
light, at present, just touches my toes.
This gladdens my heart, and much
happiness and goodness has already
begun to flow.

❋ ❋ ❋ ❋

Your Own Magical Light

When we have a dark and gloomy
 day,
Eventually the sun Breaks through
 piercing with it's golden ray.

It shimmers strong and golden
 bright,
Like dancing stars which brighten
 night.

The dark and gloom is shattered,
 now the sun is peeping through
We find the darkness never
 mattered.

So if your life, it too, is dark and
 shadows your sight.
Stop, be still and receive within your
 own magical light.

As we all have the opportunity to
 receive this heavenly light.
Which can transform the darkest of
 lives into glorious days,
Which were as dark as night.

❄ ❄ ❄ ❄

Light Up Life's Window

As you wander past houses at night
Isn't it lovely to see in a window, a
welcoming light?

That glows so brightly it gladdens
your heart?
And reminds you that from others
you are not far apart.

If you can accept pure light into your
window of life.
It will show forth from you for the
rest of your life.

For if you have light in your window
of life glowing bright.
It too, to the eye, will be a welcoming
sight.

❈ ❈ ❈ ❈

Within the Light

Do you walk . . .Within the light?
Do you hold this illumination?
Is it good and bright?

Does your light so shine, for all
to see?
Is your spirit glistening?
Is it dancing free?

Do you have a sparkle, like a
crystal, wherever you go?
Do you share its radiance with all
those you know?

Allow your light to shine, don't
hide it away.
Share it with all, let it ripple
and sway.

We all of us have our own true light
Which we do not draw upon as
often as we might.

For it is the Christ Light which
shines within.
Which brings brightness to us all
when shadows may cloud and dim.

❋ ❋ ❋ ❋

A Shower of Light and Love

Open your heart and mind to God
    above,
And in return He will shower you with
    His Light and Love.

Guiding you, drawing you, sending love
    which will uphold.
Sending peace in mind, body and spirit
    which shouldn't be left untold.

So receive His Light, may it surround
    you, draw comfort from His love.
Be glad and rejoice in it for it is
    showered upon you from God above.

❋ ❋ ❋ ❋

Let Your Light Shine

So let your light shine that it may reach
    far flung places.
So it may bring joy and enlightenment
    and illuminate dark faces.

May your light shine so it can uplift
    and bring hope to many.
May it bring peace to mind, body and
    soul, to those who hadn't any.

Allow your light to illuminate your soul
    good and bright for all to see.
So that the world and all within it
    might be uplifted and set free.

❋ ❋ ❋ ❋

Protection of Light

Golden shimmers of light and love,
Fall about me, sprinkled from above,
Spheres of white light tumble down,
And fall about me on the ground.
A rainbow of colours over arches all,
Misting and hazy, mingles with all,
They now all surround me to produce
A protection of light.
It is so warming and uplifting and
Such a wonderful sight.

❋ ❋ ❋ ❋

Little Stars

Stars of cosmic light fill my heart
Radiating love, though we may be far
apart.

That you may be aware of the power
filtering through,
Bringing their healing light and love
unto you.

These little stars are about everywhere.
They are there for us all to gather and
to share.

❋ ❋ ❋ ❋

A Flood of Colours

Colours flood from my heart for those who
are sometimes far apart.
These colours leave with warmth and love,
filtered through from God above.

The colours uplift, warm and gladden those
to whom they are sent
And reaches and guides those for whom
they are truly meant.

Tiny stars of cosmic light and colour go
forth.
Which includes love, help, enfoldment and
self worth.

So receive that to you which is sent,
And accept and welcome it in the way it is
meant.

For these stars of light and colours now
about you fall,
And will protect you and lift you should you
stumble or fall.

So move forward with joy, peace and love.
For if light and colours you have within,
your spirit will be free like a dove.

❋ ❋ ❋ ❋

Dove of Peace

Oh gentle, snow white, little dove.
Fluttering your wings of love.

Bring peace to hearts and minds,
To all those you happen to find.

Dear dove of peace and love,
Sing your cheerful tune from high
    in the sky above.

May you bring your sign of peace,
    may it last for ever.
May the ties of friendship never
    sever.

Thank you, dear dove of purity and
    light.
So gentle and loving, so full of
    might.

❅ ❅ ❅ ❅

Key of Acceptance

Here am I, waiting, and for what?
For something that may happen,
   though I know not what.

We mustn't spend our time guessing
   at what might be.
Of things that could happen to you or
   me.

Things never turn out the way we
   think they should.
Then that way we think of the way it
   could.

The secret is acceptance of the way
   things are and will be.
If this we can do, then our complete
   self may feel free.

If we can allow the key of acceptance
   to unlock our hearts.
We will find true contentment and
   peace, and our new life will start.

❈ ❈ ❈ ❈

Do You Hear Words of Wisdom?

Take time out to listen, what do you
    hear?
Do you hear words of wisdom you can
    hold dear?

For when this you are able to do,
This can bring delight and guidance
    to you.

So listen carefully and with great care,
When you first hear words within, it
    really makes you stare!

But persevere, as much joy and help
    can unfold,
Through all of this many great things
    shall be told.

The most important point is to accept
    what you hear.
Treasure this gift in your heart and
    keep it ever dear!

❋ ❋ ❋ ❋

Think of Me

Think of me if you will,
Take a little time to be still.

Send me your blessings one by
  one.
Take time to consider what will
  be done.

Share with me your heart - what
  is held within.
And decide, now is the time to
  begin.

Open you mind and share its
  thoughts with all
And listen to voices of wisdom
  as they call.

Then step forward into your new
  and colourful world.
And observe all that's yours and
  yours to yield.

Receive all that is given to you
  into your being.
This be in your feeling, doing,
  seeing.

❀ ❀ ❀ ❀

Tips for Today

Let your life on earth be full
    of worth.
Do what you can for your
    fellow man.
Give what you will, but take
    time to be still.
Always try to be kind, but
    keep a clear mind.
Be what you are, this is the
    best by far.
Try to forgive always and a
    clear conscience stays.
Treasure all that you hear,
    place it in your heart
Keep it ever dear!

❈ ❈ ❈ ❈

'Can't See Wood for Trees'

You want to look, but you can't
    see wood for trees.
And because of this, you can't
    be completely at ease.

You try to see as much as you
    can.
But still can't see it all, so you
    can't plan

Take a step back and have a
    detached view,
And very soon your trees will
    become few.

It's when you move in too close,
It's trees, not wood you see the
    most.

✳ ✳ ✳ ✳

The Pearl Within

Within an oyster, we know that
occasionally can be found nature's
gift of a pearl so pure and white.
Such a beautiful treasure, a gift of
chance, and when it's revealed
within, behold a wonderful sight!

We, unlike the oysters, **all** have a
beautiful pearl held within.
This pearl is of peace, which is held
deep in our very being – search for
it, go on begin.

As our pearl will not reveal itself
easily, for it you will have to truly
search.
It may not be easy – you may feel
at times, unbalanced – from side
to side you may lurch.

But one day you will find your pearl
of inner peace, glowing and radiant
for all to see.
And your body, mind and spirit will
be set free.

❋ ❋ ❋ ❋

The Bark of Life

Keep picking away at the bark of life
and soon the good strong trunk you
will reveal.

With patterns for you to look at and
study, and what you find beneath
will help you heal.

For you will find all you need to
know, and you will also know on
which track to go!

And once the plan you are able to
see, you will know its right, and
will wander free.

❋ ❋ ❋ ❋

Close Up, Look Within

Sometimes look within, and let all go
    on about you.
Let trouble wash past, and
    occasionally do what you want to.

For if you are a chasm, open for all to
    fall in,
This will cause much discomfort, so
    close up, look within.

Have thoughts of your own that are
    happy and good.
Don't always do all that people think
    you should.

For your mind is your own, to do with
    as you think best.
But always remember, take time to
    rest.

So try not to be affected by the sadness
    and gloom that may be around.
But if this is so, close up, look within,
    happiness can be found.

❀ ❀ ❀ ❀

A New World in our Hearts

There is a world out there that we
should all try to see,
Which grants those that look, love,
peace, light and harmony.

Not just harmony with those all
around us, each of our days,
But harmony within ourselves, that
can help in so many ways.

So try to look for that world out
there, deep within your heart.
For if you want to find it, look inside
yourself, as this is where it starts.

❀ ❀ ❀ ❀

What's for the Best

Here I sit, watching someone with
their future in their hands.
Trying and fretting, using the best
made plans.

Guide them, heavenly Lord, that
they may do your Will.
Help them and strengthen them,
allow them to be still.

So your guidance may enter their
hearts and minds.
So that they may receive true gifts
of many kinds.

Do with them, Father, as you will –
what's for the best.
And strengthen them, that they
may do the rest.

We leave it to you, dear Lord – you
know our plan.
But we know you are there if we
reach out our hand.

❄ ❄ ❄ ❄

Unwrap Your Feelings

It's always important to show you
    care.
To keep your feelings under wraps
    is hardly fair.

So say with much conviction how
    you really feel.
Explain, with love and courage,
    so all can see its real.

For if this you never do,
How will others know what goes
    on inside of you?

❋ ❋ ❋ ❋

Be What You Are!

Be what you be and you will be
    free!

But not to be yourself you will lose
    self wealth.

For the effort to pretend gets the
    better of you in the end.

So always be what you are, on your
    journey may you travel far.

And once you reach the end, you'll
    be glad you didn't pretend.

❉ ❉ ❉ ❉

What Have You?

What have you to give, in this world
in which we live,
Have you got time to share, to help
those in despair?

Have you got knowledge with which
to part,
Which could give others a little
start?

Have you got a talent which
everyone could share,
To bring joy and to show you really
care?

Have you got peace in your mind, to
radiate to those you find?

Have you got love in your heart, to
give forth to those who are falling
apart?

Do you feel you could do a little
more and this saddens your heart?
Well perhaps today we could all
make a fresh start.

❀ ❀ ❀ ❀

Outside of Yourself

Step outside of yourself, take a
   look, what do you see?

Do you see someone contained,
   struggling to be free?

Do you see someone that's happy
   or . . . . sad?

Or glowing with goodness or . . . .
   just plain bad?

Well, remember if you don't like
   what you see.

You can change, you know!
   just say, "It's up to me!"

❄ ❄ ❄ ❄

Fire of Desire

Do you have deep within, a
glowing fire?
Which warms and flickers and
brings forth desire?

Do you have so much you want to
do - for which you are yearning?
This is, indeed, what keeps the
fire burning!

Never let this fire of desire burn
right out.
As all your aims will be no more,
there will be less to think about.

So always desire something, deep
within your heart.
And eventually you'll experience
much pleasure, which will touch
your every part.

✻ ✻ ✻ ✻

Use All You Have

Do you use all your talents that you
have within?
Or do you push them aside because
you're scared to begin?

Perhaps you are frightened of failing,
not getting it right first time?
But to let something like that stop
you would be a crime!

All things take time to perfect and
eventually achieve.
All you need is patience, courage and
to in yourself believe.

Step forward and no longer be shy!
Use your gifts and talents so that
others might know why.

✳ ✳ ✳ ✳

Are Your Roots Well Spread?

Are your roots firmly embedded in
     the ground?
Are you happy with the surroundings
     that you've found?

Will you ever be uprooted and
     planted in another spot?
Or will you stay put, whether happy
     or not?

But if you're happily situated and
     your roots are well spread.
Console yourself, look upwards, raise
     your weary head.

As if you are truly settled in body,
     soul and mind.
Your roots will spread further and
     more stability you will find.

❊ ❊ ❊ ❊

Body, Soul and Mind

Do you ever consider your body, soul
and mind?
Do you ever take the time, to all three
to be kind?

Yes! you say, I look after my body very
well!
I exercise it, keep it clean and feed it,
can't you tell?

But how about the other - say your
mind?
Do you test it, question it and see
what you can find?

How about your soul, do you consider
it, although it you cannot see?
Do you allow it to wander and prepare
to set it free?

For remember, if you can, there's
more to us all than meets the eye!
There's more than physical and
material - so endeavour to nurture
them - go on! Why not try?

❋ ❋ ❋ ❋

A Private Journey

Days come, days go,
They fly past - this we know.

Days quickly run into weeks,
And have we achieved that which
we dearly seek?

Or have we been absorbed with the
practical and mundane,
And from this we begin to feel the
strain?

We, all of us, need a release from
our earthly life,
That rewards us with love, light
and peace and no strife.

This should be a private journey
for just you or me,
When your mind can wander, and
your heart is free.

So have time and thoughts that are
just your very own,
Where you are free and happy and
are truly alone.

❋ ❋ ❋ ❋

Holidays of Your Mind

If you don't have a holiday, why not
just have one in your mind?
Within it you can travel anywhere, it's
surprising the places you can find.

The travels of the mind are unlimitless,
you can go where you wish.
There's no cares and worries - no buses
to miss!

You can take your time and travel at
your own pace.
You can do as you want, even feel the
wind in your face.

Your mind is yours to use and explore
with just as you like.
So visualise and picture, and in your
mind see all the sights.

✳ ✳ ✳ ✳

One Thing at a Time

Try to think of one thing at a time.
Concentrate fully on that thing in
your mind.

Look at it from every point of view.
Think of each problem like this
and soon the many will seem few.

For when you approach your
difficulties in these ways.
The big becomes small and only
the important stays.

✻ ✻ ✻ ✻

Clouds of Thought

Do thoughts float through your
mind?
Like the white clouds in the sky
we find.

Some clouds hold rain, which
sometimes comes pouring down.
Other clouds are just passing
through, at them there's no need
to frown.

Allow your thoughts to be like
these and let them float by and
have nothing to say.
Do not dwell on dark clouds of
thought, let them pass and float
away.

❇ ❇ ❇ ❇

Your Book Cover

No matter what we look like, it's
inside of us which counts.
No matter whether we are a little
out of shape and could lose the
odd ounce.

It makes no difference whether
we're fat or thin, short or tall.
It's your thinking, your attitude,
how you live, sharing your life with
all.

It's your inner self which truly
counts and is the real you.
As this will travel through eternity
and help you through.

So be happy and content within,
never mind your looks!
After all you never choose a book
solely by how the cover looks!

❄ ❄ ❄ ❄

Don't Just Sit There!

Don't sit in your chair and just despair.
Get out for a while, pass a shop window
    and smile.

Why not pop into the neighbour next
    door?
Why not take her a picture you want no
    more?

Why not write to Uncle Jim?
Or pick up the phone and talk to Auntie
    Min?

Why not thank the milkman with a
    cheery grin?
Why not thank the postman for popping
    the mail in?

There is so much we can do.
Rather than sit and just let life come to
    you.

So just don't sit there in your lonely
    chair.
Get out there and share, show people
    you care!

✳ ✳ ✳ ✳

Smile

When life gets you down,
Just don't sit and frown.

Get out for a while,
And to every person, give a
  broad smile.

For it's the frown which gets
  you down,
And the smile which makes
  life worth while!

❋ ❋ ❋ ❋

A Good Laugh

Do you benefit from the wonderful
    tonic of laughter?
Do you laugh and giggle until you're
    quite out of breath for well after?

A good hearty laugh is helpful to
    mind and soul.
It refreshes you and sort of cleanses,
    and then you feel whole.

Because when you laugh you let
    yourself go.
You're full of happiness and fun and
    you don't care who knows.

Don't be reluctant to laugh, never
    stifle a giggle!
It's not good to do this as
    uncomfortably we would wriggle!

So go on and have a good old
    fashioned laugh, let yourself go!
If you are happy and fun loving why
    not let it show?

❊ ❊ ❊ ❊

Put a Smile on Your Face

If you don't know what to do with
your face.
Why not put a smile on it and
brighten up the place?

For a smile is like a boomerang,
you always get one back!
For if you smile at someone, you
very often get one back.

So why not try to make the world a
more cheerful place?
Go on, be daring, and put a smile
upon your face!

❋ ❋ ❋ ❋

Be Ye Joyful in All That Ye Have

Oh to be in love,
And be free like a dove.

Oh to have peace of mind,
Like this true contentment we find.

Oh to have gladness in our hearts,
To find this throughout life in every part.

Oh to have dear friends by your side,
Like this you have someone in which to
confide.

Oh to have all of these things,
It truly makes my heart sing.

Be ye joyful in all that ye have!

❋ ❋ ❋ ❋

An Empty Void

Does your life feel sometimes, like
an empty void?
Do you become disillusioned and
maybe even annoyed?

Life seems empty, pointless, like
there's nothing on offer for you.
You feel things just aren't going
your way, the good times are all
too few.

At times like these we need to pick
ourselves up and dust ourselves
down.
And replace with a big broad smile,
that gloomy old frown.

As we need to look at life
positively, right from the heart.
Remove all that is negative and
make a fresh start.

Try not to look inwards, always at
yourself.
Look outwards to others and hold
out a hand, and you will find true
wealth.

The wealth of love and compassion
within your soul.
That in time shall fill your void and
you will feel whole.

❋ ❋ ❋ ❋

The Fire

As I gaze in the fire, what do I
  see?
Glowing little faces smiling back
  at me.
Orange and golden glimmering
  and free.

Little figures darting here and
  there.
Bouncing back and forth without
  a care.
Plenty to see when I stop and
  stare.

Embers are now glowing low.
Guess it's nearing the end of the
  show.
So wistfully it's off to bed we go!

❈ ❈ ❈ ❈

A Drop in the Ocean

Look upon your day as a drop in
the ocean of life.
Remember this as you struggle
through and have to handle strife.

For your life is an ocean with
changing tides.
Waves of joy and strife will wash
about your sides.

Your day is just a drop which
dissolves into the seas of your
lifetime.
So if you've experienced a better
day than this, allow it to be
washed from your mind.

❋ ❋ ❋ ❋

When Day Meets Night

It is the time when day meets
night.
Views and landscapes slip out of
sight.

The bright blue sky is now
replaced by one that is as black
as ink.
One wonders how this
transformation comes about, it
really makes me think.

The moon is big and bright,
drifting high and free.
As I gaze at it, I wonder is it really
smiling at me?

Surrounding it are many glittering
stars, shining like chips of
twinkling glass.
How magical I find this scene,
once more I ask, "How did this all
come to pass?"

All I can guess is the Lord gave us
day and also night.
So when the day is ending, be
glad you see this fascinating sight.

Remember at this time, there is
nothing to cause you fright.
It's simply the part of the day we
all call night!

❊ ❊ ❊ ❊

The Star Studded Blanket

Night time draws closer as the
evening shadows fall.
And soon a blanket of star studded
darkness will cover over all.

Helping us so to sleep and in turn
take our rest.
So when we rise the following morn,
we feel at our best.

Cool and calming moonlight falls
against the window pane.
Such a soothing light, there's nothing
quite the same.

So be at peace with all and yourself
as you lay in your bed.
Let dreams of beauty drift in, as you
rest your weary head.

❋ ❋ ❋ ❋

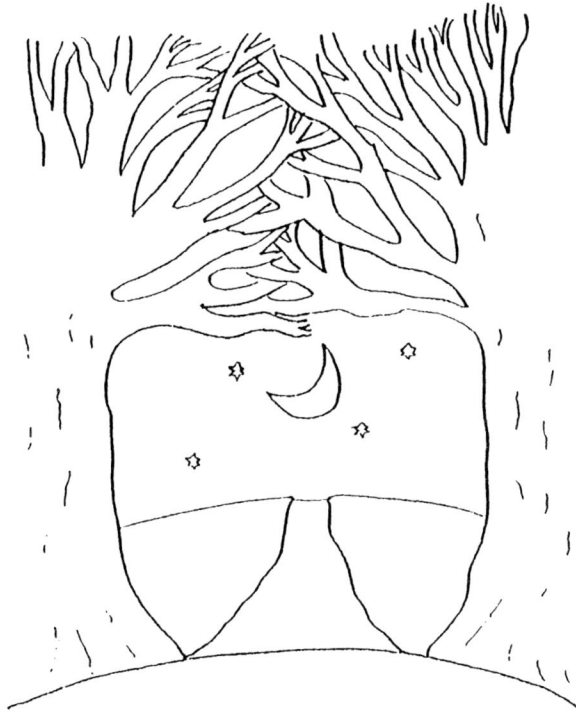

A New Day Tomorrow

Try not to ponder on the day that
you've had.
Let it go, don't look back on it and
feel so sad.

But look forward with hope, to
your new day tomorrow.
A fresh day! A new day! without
any sorrow.

So rest your head upon your
pillow and sleep.
And ask that the angels may you
in safety keep.

❀ ❀ ❀ ❀

Bed Time

When I settle down to sleep,
I ask that you will us in safety
    keep.

That we will wake once again next
    morn,
Refreshed, awakened, even
    re–born.

But in the meantime grant us
    peaceful rest,
Because above all that can help
    us, sleep is best.

❋ ❋ ❋ ❋

When I Pray

Lord when I settle down to pray.
I sometimes find it difficult to
know what to say.
The easiest of all is, "Thank you
for today."

For during the day, I felt your help
assurance and love.
Your guiding hand touching from
above.
Helping me along, when I needed
a little shove.

Next I need to say, "Sorry for the
wrong things I've done."
Your forgiveness I always seek to
find, one to one.
Along the awkward track of life
which winds beneath the Sun.

After this I ask your blessings
upon my family and friends.
And ask for them, that their
trouble mends.
And apologise, Lord, for the list
which never ends.

But I know if I forget the things I
should say.
That you understand me most
when I pray.
So now I end with "Amen" if I may.

✳ ✳ ✳ ✳

Thank You Letter

As with when we write a thank
you letter, we end it 'with much
love'.
We must too, end our day with
this parting phrase to our God
above.

Along with this we could give our
thanks for that very day.
To thank the Father for His help,
which He sent to us in many
different ways.

For surely God too, would draw
great pleasure from the occasional
thank you letter.
And perhaps by sending love and
giving thanks, we too will feel a
little better.

❀ ❀ ❀ ❀

Lead Me to Dream Land

May I sleep peacefully now in my
    bed.
And to dream land may I be
    led.

Where things are whole and
    perfect in every way.
Where I need do nothing and have
    little to say.

Where only good and peaceful
    events come about.
Where all is quiet, where no one
    shouts.

Lead me to this glorious and
    tranquil place.
So I may wake in the morn with a
    smile upon my face.

❋ ❋ ❋ ❋

Uphold Me in My Darkness

May the Lord carry me safely to
where I am going.
Where this may be there's no way
of knowing.

Guide me along on my sweet way.
Upholding me and drawing me
each of my days.

Blow me along like a summer's
breeze.
So I might meet each challenge
with great ease.

Encourage and praise me when I
do good.
And advise me again if I don't do
as I should.

For knowing you are there by my
side.
Will uphold me in times of
darkness, dear Lord, my ever
faithful guide.

❋ ❋ ❋ ❋

Sleep Gently

Sleep gently in your bed,
Rest upon your pillow every hair
of your head.

Let you mind wander far away,
Where angels sing and fairies
play.

Let your heart be open, so love
and gentleness can pour in.
May it be filled with loveliness to
its brim.

Rest your soul and body, let cares
and worries flee away.
Sleep and be filled with peace, so
you are ready for another day.

✻ ✻ ✻ ✻

Your Fairy Castle

Can you see a fairy castle in
your mind?
Where all is peaceful, caring
and kind?

Where moonlight shines and
makes it shimmer.
And stars twinkle and glimmer.

Pretty lights from it's windows
glow.
Dusky dancing shadows they
throw.

Such love and tranquillity are
radiated from such a place.
That bring joy and reflection to
your heart and a smile upon
your face.

So wander up to this castle in
your mind.
There you can escape and pure
delight you will find.

❉ ❉ ❉ ❉

Aware of Another Day Dawning

As you wake each and every morning;
Are you aware of another day
dawning?

Do you take time to be still?
And think of your day, how it you will
fill?

Are you as your day does progress,
aware of it, do you watch it unfold?
For if this you do, you'll observe things
which might have remained untold.

Because if you rush, with your head
hung down.
There's much you'll miss, life will seem
dull and you may frown.

But if you walk through each day
noticing and watching all that's before
you.
A smile will pass your lips, gladness
will fill your heart and your troubles
will seem few!

❄ ❄ ❄ ❄

Love Starts in Your Heart

Love is a strange thing, sometimes you
can't see it, but you know it's there.
It's in the unspoken word or in a little
glance, but you know that love exists
true and fair.

Even though you can feel love
surrounding you, do you have it deep
within your heart?
For this is where it really matters, it's
from there love should make a start.

For if you have this warm, glowing
feeling in your heart, it filters through.
You will radiate that same feeling, no
matter where you go, it will always
shine through.

❉ ❉ ❉ ❉

You

Oh my love, come to me,
For I know you are there.
Watching over me,
Seeing I am free.

You breath upon me, inspire me,
So I know what I might be.
You open my eyes,
That I might see.

You open my heart,
So I may start.
You uplift my soul,
So I may feel whole.

You enlighten my mind,
So that I might find.
You cleanse my thoughts,
That I might be taught.

You guide and love me,
I feel, but do not see.
May blessings be upon us,
Both you and me.

❋ ❋ ❋ ❋

I Know You are There

Love and guide me as along life's road
I tread.
Help me to understand situations and
things that have been said.

Lead me, so I may not stumble or fall.
But if I do, catch me, uplift me so that
I may again stand tall.

Just to know you are there every step
of the way.
Many cares and worries this simply
allays.

Never leave me – although I know you
never will.
As you will help me, and my life
together we will fulfil.

I give you thanks for being there, for
being near by.
Because I know whatever happens
you'll be there by my side.

❋ ❋ ❋ ❋

Someone by Your Side

Do you sometimes feel as if you are not
alone, that you have someone by your
side?
Although you are on your own, you are
aware of a presence, have you thought,
it could be God as your guide?

At first this revelation is breathtaking,
and to say the least a bit of a surprise.
But once you accept His presence and
become aware of His help, much joy
from this does arise.

So be sure to remember that you always
have at your side, a very good and dear
friend.
And when allowed to advise and guide
you, will bring you joy and peace
without end.

✳ ✳ ✳ ✳

The Hand of God

Do you sometimes feel the hand of God
has touched you, you get a tickle down
your spine?
Perhaps things aren't going well, then
suddenly everything is fine.

From a cloudy sky, do you find a ray of
sunshine breaks through?
It warms you and uplifts you as it's
touching you.

In a silent hour do the birds begin to
sing?
And to your heart and mind great
pleasure do they bring?

It's these special times when the hand
of God reaches out and touches you.
And transforms your sky of darkness,
into one of bright blue.

❋ ❋ ❋ ❋

God The Healer

At some time in our lives, may we all
be blessed by the Power of Healing.
The peace and love which gives us
such a wonderful feeling.

This is a feeling which comes as
refreshing, warming, glowing.
Which is channelled from God above
unto us, sometimes without us
knowing.

All of us deep within, have the ability
not only to heal but to be healed.
It is, indeed, granted from God and
with His love it is sealed.

To heal and to be healed is a matter
of simple acceptance deep within.
To open up your heart and mind and
let God the Healer in.

❋ ❋ ❋ ❋

Healing Touch

I thank you for that healing
  touch,
Which helps so very, very
  much.

Although you probably don't
  even know,
Because I guess I rarely let it
  show.

But it really matters deep
  down,
And places a smile, where
  there's been a frown.

So thank you for that gentle
  healing touch,
Which really helps, so very,
  very much.

❅ ❅ ❅ ❅

Heavenly Healing Lord

Dear heavenly healing Lord, I
know you come to me.
You bring peace to my mind, you
open my eyes that I might see.

You bring love in my heart,
which radiates good and true.
You cleanse my thinking, so my
troubles become few.

You breathe new life upon my
very soul.
Comforting and caring, and
wonderfully, I feel whole.

Dear heavenly healing Lord, I
know you come to me.
You walk hand in hand with me,
through joy and adversity.

So finally I thank you from the
very bottom of my heart.
For I know Your gentle healing,
can touch our every part.

❋ ❋ ❋ ❋

78

Just Another Short Snatch

If you wake up feeling blue.
Think of all the nice things that
lay ahead of you.

Think of good things – not bad.
Try to be happy – not sad.

Even if you think today may not
be your best.
Although you may not think so,
it will pass like all the rest.

Today is just another short snatch
in your life itself.
With many experiences, full of
untold wealth.

It is true, you may stumble or fall.
But give thanks and count your
blessings, big or small.

❋ ❋ ❋ ❋

God's Plan

Do you sometimes ask the
question, "Why has God let this
awful thing come about?"
A thing that is so dreadful, you
want to shut it out.

From sad and tragic events, very
often there are lessons to be
learnt.
We can't accept this straight
away, but at the time we realise
it's true and wish it weren't.

All things are sent for a reason,
be they good or bad.
Whether they make us happy, or
indeed make us sad.

Try to accept all that is placed
before you, try to understand.
As although we can't see it, it's
all part of God's Plan.

❀ ❀ ❀ ❀

A Rare and Precious Feeling

Occasionally when something happens,
does it touch deep within your heart?
Is it something that somehow, from the
rest is set apart?

Yet you know not really why that
feeling should come to you.
As it's a rare and precious feeling,
which happens all too few.

It may be a child's drawing, given to
you with lots of love.
It may be a clasp of a hand, a gentle
touch of love.

Maybe it's a little card to say, "Thinking
of you."
Or a pretty bunch of flowers
spontaneously handed to you.

Whatever it is that happens, which
touches your heart within.
Behold these lovely gifts and treasure
them as memories never dim.

❋ ❋ ❋ ❋

Hidden Gems

Do you sometimes despair, and
cry, "Is life never fair? Why has
this happened to me? Why do I
sometimes look but do not see?"

"Is this problem ever going to
disappear? Will I never get over
this terrible fear? Will I ever find
someone to love?"

But if these questions you some-
times ask, then you're having
lessons that won't forever last.

Within each of these feelings there
is hidden a gem. From which you
will learn; so the same thing won't
happen again.

❈ ❈ ❈ ❈

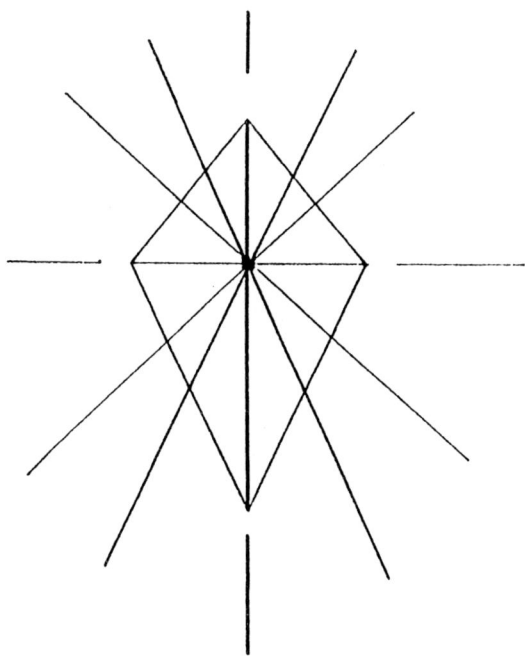

Life's Wonders

Life has many wonders left untold.
Some of them new, some of them
old.

There are many things we don't
understand.
Which we sometimes discuss with
our fellow man.

How does this work, why does it
happen?
Why does it sicken, why does it
sadden?

Where do we come from, where
do we go?
All of the answers, we want to
know.

I guess if we can't answer all of
these.
We must just accept – what will
be, will be.

❈ ❈ ❈ ❈

An Inner Strength

There is an inner strength we all
have, which we need from time to
time.
We need it when we have trouble,
or a problem, or when things just
don't turn out fine.

We don't know where this feeling
comes from, at times such as
these.
But it surges up inside us and
carries us along, rather like a
summer's breeze.

❃ ❃ ❃ ❃

Raise Up Your Eyes from the Road

People are rushing to do this or that,
This I am watching whilst I'm sat.

Each with cares and worries of their own.
Worries, perhaps, about work or maybe at
home.

They are so wrapped up with what
troubles them most.
They perhaps don't notice any good to
toast.

But if only they stopped and raised their
eyes from the road,
And took time out to observe those things
so very often untold.

To notice the beauty of flowers, plants or
even a bee,
Or gaze at the sky or take a look at a tree.

All these sights would gladden their heart.
Because if we notice all the good around,
it provides a sound base from which to
start.

❊ ❊ ❊ ❊

Just Like a Kitten

Have you ever seen a kitten
standing on a wall?
He considers whether to jump,
but he's frightened he might fall.

Then suddenly off he hops,
landing safely on the ground.
And scampers off to explore the
new surroundings he has found.

We too, are just like the kitten.
We don't know whether to take a
chance.
We too, would want to know, "Will
we land on our feet?" in advance.

But sometimes, like the kitten,
We must trust our instincts and
jump.
We may land safe and sound, or
perhaps with a little bump.

But no matter which it is that
happens to us when we fall.
Either way we will learn from it, so
it's better to jump than not at all.

And rather like the kitten, when
we jump from our wall.
We don't know what wonders lie
beyond, that could well change it
all.

✳ ✳ ✳ ✳

A Bridge in the Distance

There is, in the distance, a bridge
in sight,
Which has running beneath it,
precious water, shimmering in the
light.

Is the bridge my next important
step?
Is this where my dreams shall be
met?

For perhaps I should use the
bridge to reach the far side,
And use it as direction and allow
it to be my guide.

But will I use the bridge?
Well, I guess it's up to me.
Do I have the confidence to be free
or trust, what will be will be?

❊   ❊   ❊   ❊

Think Not in Years . . But in Days

My birthday comes and my birthday goes.
"How old am I?" No one really knows.

For much life has passed before we
reached this place.
So let peace fill your heart, and a smile
come to your face.

Try to think, "I'm not a year older, but a
year closer to the next step!"
So don't think of yourself as old, don't
think of your age, try to forget.

It doesn't matter what your age is, it's how
young you feel in your heart that counts.
Don't tot-up the years – it's not the
amount

Just feel happy and glad, at the years that
you've had.
Try to live and love and rejoice in many
ways, think not in years, but just in days.

✳ ✳ ✳ ✳

Is Your Real Life Passing You By?

Do you find there are not enough hours in
a day?
"I don't know where to start!" Is that what
you sometimes say?

Do the jobs and chores mount up, does it
seem never ending?
What first will it be, cooking, ironing or
mending?

But as the list of jobs gets longer.
Why not take a little time out to ponder?

All these jobs are just things that will keep.
So don't fret over them, no matter how big
the heap.

There's more to life than housework and
shopping to buy.
As when you're doing this, your real life is
passing you by.

So why not spread out your jobs over a
number of days?
And then like this you can enjoy yourself
too, in many other ways.

❈ ❈ ❈ ❈

The Door to My Future

The door to my future lays before
me.
It won't be long before I can step
through and be free.

It is dark and heavy and at present,
just ajar.
But as the door opens wider, I look
forward to seeing afar.

For beyond this door, lie wonders
untold.
Wonderful shades of all colours
before me will unfold.

These colours are already seeping
through the opened door.
Laying gently before me, falling
about me upon the floor.

So I wait with excitement for the
door to be flung open wide.
So I may pass through the doorway
and be surrounded by the light
which lays on the other side.

❋ ❋ ❋ ❋

There Are Times

There are times in life that are
rough.
These are times we should try to
be tough.

There are times that are sad, that
make us cry.
These are times when we ask
ourselves "Why?"

There are times when life feels
difficult and mundane.
These are times when we feel the
strain.

But there are also good times for
which we must thank.
And forget the sad times to which
we sank.

There are times which bring
happiness for us to remember.
These times are placed in our
hearts as glowing embers.

There are times when we feel so
good, we feel we could fly.
At times like this we could reach
out and touch the sky.

There are so many times when
happiness and gladness fill our
hearts.
We should try to remember this
before sadness makes a start.

❈ ❈ ❈ ❈

Like a Candle

We, like a candle, could light up a
room.
We could light up our lives and those
around us - why not start, and soon?

The flame glimmers and flickers,
dancing silhouettes across the wall.
It stands before us, shining bright
and tall.

Before this, the candle stands alone
in the dark - it can't be seen.
But when we strike a match and
touch it's wick, light from it does
beam.

We can be like the candle, standing
isolated in the dark.
But if we allow ourselves to be held
in the light, we too will have a
flickering flame deep within our
heart.

✳ ✳ ✳ ✳

You Are What You Are

You are what you are,
Be it cleaner or movie star.

I am what I am,
Just say, "I can, I can."

I do what I do,
And I see it through.

I feel what I feel
And I know it's real.

I think what I think,
I don't need a shrink.

I know what I know,
And eventually it will show!

✻ ✻ ✻ ✻

Stand Up and Be Counted

There comes a time in life, when you
must stand up and be counted.
Even though you're worried that by
some you might be doubted.

For if you fall into this tempting trap
of concern.
You will withhold joy from others, for
which they dearly yearn.

So go on with faith, courage and
hope in your heart.
For the time is now here when you
should start.

❋ ❋ ❋ ❋

Come Out from Your Shell

Share what you have in your mind
with others, don't be shy!
Do this that I ask of you, there's no
need to ask "Why?"

It's important that you let the talents
you have show.
That you share what you do, so that
others might know!

So come out from your shell, and
face the world which is waiting.
Be forthright and bold, stop
hesitating.

❀ ❀ ❀ ❀

Never Lose Sight of Your Dreams

We can all see our dreams out if we
really try.
But they have to be worked at and
kept in our mind's eye.

We have to concentrate upon our
goal or aim.
And if at first we don't succeed, we
should try again.

As if you truly want something,
whatever it may be.
With time and effort soon good fruits
you will see.

But never loose sight of your dream,
no matter what it is.
Never loose faith in the fact - one
day it could exist.

❄ ❄ ❄ ❄

So Much to Learn

The trials of life seem, sometimes never
ending.
Troubles, worries and problems that all
need mending.

From all of these precious times we can
learn so very much.
We learn forgiveness, love, compassion
and these our heart does touch.

Our lives will always be fulfilled if these
things we find.
Because we will appreciate the peace it
brings to the mind.

So we must try to learn from our
problems and feel enriched by them all.
As from these we will learn, rather like
a child after a fall.

❋ ❋ ❋ ❋

Tapestry of Life

Why am I who I am, why a woman,
why not a man?
Why do I live here and not in
Lincolnshire?

Why was I born in '64, why wasn't I
born the year before.
How come I can do this, but can't do
that?

How come I'm not stood up, how
come I'm sat?
Why am I well built and dark, why
aren't I always up to the mark?

Well none of us know really, why we
are here.
We just know we must learn, and
hold our lessons dear.

For all of these are stitches of the
tapestry of life.
Stitches of happiness, joy and of
strife.

❋ ❋ ❋ ❋

A Lesson from a Fall

So much can happen in such a
short time.
As we start a new day - who
knows what we'll find?

People, places, faces all change,
sometimes as quick as that!
Things never remain the same,
since we last had a chat.

But as we grow older, we learn we
cannot change this - we must
accept.
That things do change faster then
we would like, so we should learn
not to fret.

Each experience has its teachings
for us all.
So there is always a lesson to be
learnt from a fall!

❉ ❉ ❉ ❉

Changes in Our Lives

I feel refreshed, renewed and alive
    once more.
So much different than I did before.

All of us in our lives, have changes
    which come about.
Which comfort and protect us, that
    push away doubt.

We learn and digest the events that
    have passed.
And remember answers to questions
    that we asked.

From all of this we learn so very much.
From experience, simple words and a
    gentle touch.

All of these happenings are bound to
    alter us in some ways.
Giving a little wisdom, renewing our
    hopes - changing our days.

So try to feel refreshed and renewed
    from which you've learned.
And receive the comfort and joy for
    this you have truly earned.

❋ ❋ ❋ ❋

We All Change

We none of us remain the same
person our whole life through.
We change, we progress and learn
from all which we do.

We learn many lessons in the
course of our lives.
And consequently we all change -
families, friends, husbands, wives.

So don't be disillusioned if those
around you have changed.
For it is merely progression and
cannot be rearranged.

❋ ❋ ❋ ❋

The Coin of Fate

Sometimes things happen in life
we cannot change.
No matter how we plan, or try to
arrange.

At these times no matter what,
things still go wrong.
It is at these unfortunate times
when we should try to be strong.

We should try to understand what
life dishes up.
Remembering it is fate, not we
ourselves, that places us in the
position in which we are stuck.

So please don't blame yourself
needlessly when things don't run
to plan.
As all of us have in life, times
when fate takes a hand.

But remember, fate, like a coin,
has another side too.
And as the coin of fate takes a
turn, only good will come to you.

❋ ❋ ❋ ❋

The Boat of Life

Stand firm, although the boat
   of life may sway.
With feet firmly on the ground,
   no matter what others say.

For you know what you know.
And given time, this will show.

So be patient until the time is
   right.
Then all will be well in everyone's
   sight.

❋ ❋ ❋ ❋

Shining Example

You have taken what fate has given you,
    right on the chin.
You have steered a course where some
    would not know where to begin.

You have stood firm and weathered the
    storm.
Even though life at times, must have felt
    like a piercing thorn.

We all of us admire your faith, courage
    and hope.
You are a shining example of how with
    trouble to cope.

It has sometimes been difficult to know
    what to say.
But one thing you can be sure of, for you
    we always pray.

The compliment, 'A Shining Example' is
    not just for you.
It is of course, for your family too.

For the way you have coped and handled
    your strife.
Is something I shall remember for the rest
    of my life.

✳ ✳ ✳ ✳

Life's Merry-go-round

Life is like a merry-go-round, and
    sometimes you want to get off.
But the more you try the faster it
    goes, it just won't seem to stop.

Pictures and images go flashing
    and racing by.
So quickly your life is passing you
    by.

But as you ride on life's
    merry-go-round.
Treasure all within that you've
    found.

Look straight ahead at what's
    coming up.
Not from side to side - like that
    you'll feel you're stuck!

❋ ❋ ❋ ❋

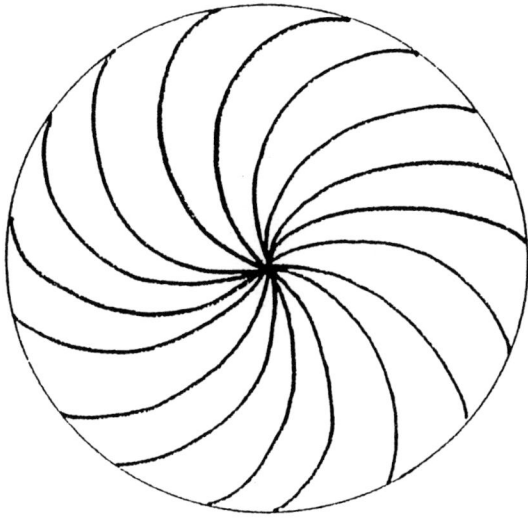

Life's Dish

Life is sometimes hard, we all have
to admit that things aren't always
as we would wish.
But sometimes we have to accept
that which is placed upon life's
dish.

For all that is placed before us
isn't all that we would like.
But we have to accept the portion
placed before us, and do with it
what we might.

As with the dish of life, it is at
times bitter-sweet.
But with time we will find a reason
why we were served with
situations we couldn't swallow,
and in turn did not eat.

You see with bitter-sweet or sweet
and sour, they do compliment
each other.
And this is the same with life's
happiness and troubles - you can't
have one without the other.

✻ ✻ ✻ ✻

The Map of Life

Thank you for my life, for it is a
happy one.
Waiting with excitement for the things
to come.
And grateful too for what has been
done.
But help me Lord, to walk not run.

For amongst the map of life,
One has to accept some strife.
So stride the problems with
conviction.
And never speculate, as this is fiction.

Meet each difficulty with hope and
common sense.
Be sure not to talk any nonsense.
If you think with a cool, calm head,
Your problems will go and you'll be
happy instead.

So remember as life passes you by.
It's far nicer to laugh rather than cry.
Just try your best to understand,
And endeavour to love your fellow
man.

❋ ❋ ❋ ❋

Thoughts and Awareness from High in the Sky

Have you been locked up inside
of you?
Do you feel as if you're struggling
free?
Things are unravelling, are you
beginning to see?

Do you realise there is more to you
than meets the eye?
Thoughts and awareness from high
in the sky.
Sometimes you feel as if you could
fly.

Is there a warmth in your hands
you can't explain?
A glowing in your heart, a beautiful
feeling to gain.
Is there a comforting feeling
spreading over your frame?

Do you have wonderful friends by
your side?
To steer you through and be your
guide.
To help you along the journey you
ride.

Do you feel as if wonders are being
offered to you on a plate?
To pass them up would be a pitiful
mistake.
But I know a big effort we shall
have to make.

It will take time, I know it will.
It won't be all flat going,
There will be the odd hill.
But to feel the light all about us
will be such a thrill.

❀ ❀ ❀ ❀

You Will Wander In from the Cold

Do you know where you're going,
indeed where you have been?
Do you know what you're going to
do, can you remember what you've
seen?

Do you feel you are drifting,
wandering in a wilderness, do you
feel alone?
Do you feel detached, solitary,
although you have no place of your
very own?

Well, one day you shall wander in
from the cold.
And you shall have what you have
longed for, and it you will have to
hold.

❀ ❀ ❀ ❀

The Corridor of Life

Life is like a corridor with, oh so
    many doors.
It lingers on before you, into the
    distance it soars.

Behind these doors are hidden
    many wondrous things.
Beyond some lay hardships, and
    beyond others angels sing.

So some doors will open unto you,
    and others will remain shut.
Some will shock and surprise you,
    and move you out of a rut.

Some doors will stick and will need
    an extra push.
Some will open with such ease,
    and in you will quickly rush.

But at the end of the corridor lies a
    door off afar.
And this is the one we will find
    ajar.

And this is the door with new life
    beyond.
Such a sobering thought of which
    to be fond.

So pace along your corridor with
hope in your heart.
For each step you take plays an
important part.

❋ ❋ ❋ ❋

The Tunnels of Life

When you walk through a tunnel,
It's rather like water passing through
a funnel.

There's only one way out, you cannot
turn about.
You must push on, you must not
doubt.

Life has it's dark tunnels which are
not too good.
But you know you must pass through
them, you know you should.

When that tunnel comes to an end.
Light surrounds you, things begin to
mend.

So when through life's tunnels you
pass.
When you reach the end, you receive a
feeling none can surpass.

Because even though perhaps you can't
see it, the light is always there.
It is all about, ready for us to share.

✻ ✻ ✻ ✻

Hands of a Clock

Have you ever watched the hands
on a clock go round?
Don't they take a long time - is
this what you've found?

Time is a precious gift for us all to
use as best we can.
So why not no longer watch the
clock, but instead perhaps you
could help your fellow man?

For life is for living, loving, sharing
and giving.
So fill each moment with a kind
thought, and these believe in.

Because by the way we think, we
can turn our lives upside down.
We can be responsible for our
happiness just by choosing to
smile instead of frown.

✳ ✳ ✳ ✳

The Bull of Life

There comes a time when you
must take the bull of life by the
horns.
Even when by doing this, it feels
like grasping thorns.

There is a time in life when this
you must do.
Else later on this will keep on
troubling you!

Because if, with your challenge
you don't succeed.
On with your life you will still
proceed.

But if your challenges turn out
just right.
Think how glad you'd feel for
putting up the fight.

For life is not only for living,
sharing and giving.
It's for trying, hoping and maybe
succeeding.

But not to try is to never know,
What you have inside that you
could show!

All of us has something to give.
So let's make the most of it and
really live!

* * * *

Time for Others and for You

It's a funny old world in which
we live.
So many people like to take,
but so few to give.

It's not money I speak of, which
we can give whilst sat.
It's time and energy, giving
that.

For even if you don't have a fat
piggy bank.
You can still do much that
people will thank.

Fill your time as much as you
can.
Try and spend some of it
helping your fellow man.

Time is precious, something
money can't buy.
So use it wisely, and try not to
sigh.

Give your time to one another.
Family, friends, neighbours, try
to cover.

But amongst all of this keep
time for you.
To think of things that you
want to.

Because some of the time you
need to unwind.
So take time out to think lovely
thoughts in your mind.

❉ ❉ ❉ ❉

Glorious Reminders

There it stands, silhouetted
against the cold grey sky.
As you gaze at it you often wonder
"Why?"

This is the church of which I talk.
That my eyes fall upon whilst I
walk.

There it has stood for hundreds of
years.
Calming and soothing many of our
fears.

We must give thanks to those who
built it so long ago.
Who have helped to leave these
buildings that we might know.

As these wonderful structures are
glorious reminders for us all.
So we might all be aware of God's
presence if we stumble or fall.

❄ ❄ ❄ ❄

Who Can We Count On?

Do not look too far into the future,
to see what it has to hold.
For many things lay before you,
and some are best left untold.

For none of us knows what the
future has in store.
Sadness or happiness, misfortune
or luck, of this we can't be sure.

The only thing we know we can
count on, is the Light and Love
God has to give.
Which is always there for us,
whether we take or give whilst we
live.

❈ ❈ ❈ ❈

Life's True Gifts

Do you think about love and caring?
The beauty of friendship and sharing?

Or do you think more about items and
cash?
Say caviar instead of bangers and
mash?

The value of life's true gifts is without
measure.
It's the true feelings of the heart that
we must treasure.

As no matter who we are, we all of us
have these.
So wonderful and warming for us they
please.

So remember no matter your monetary
worth.
That is not the reason you were placed
here on earth.

We are all of us here to learn the true
meaning of living.
To help us with this practice, loving,
sharing, caring and giving.

❋ ❋ ❋ ❋

Life's Book

My life to me, seems like a book.
Every day is like a page at which
to look.

As each day has within it
something from which we can
learn.
Sometimes so obvious as the
page we turn.

Our Birthdays are like chapters
of life's so rich and enlightening
book.
They mark the end of our year
and a new beginning at which to
look.

Each chapter is never like the
last, the characters though are
usually the same.
But sometimes, things, people,
places, do have to change.

So read life's book with hope,
love and great care.
As so much is contained within
it, which sometimes we don't
realise was there.

And eventually you arrive at the
page marked 'The End'.
But in life's book this page
means more than this, as our
book never really ends.

It means we simply turn over yet
another page.
And step forward and read on
into a different age.

✳ ✳ ✳ ✳

Heavenly Seven

What's so fascinating about
   number seven?
All I can guess it's because it
   rhymes with heaven.

For if every time we see number
   seven.
We lifted our hearts and we
   thought of Heaven. . . .

What a lovely reminder number
   seven would be.
For it would always remind us
   there is eternity.

✳ ✳ ✳ ✳

Aeroplane Ride

Oh! aeroplane way up high in the sky.
Where is it you are going to, where do
you fly?

Leaving your snow white trail behind you.
So we can trace your path in the sky so
blue.

But where do you go when you disappear
from sight?
Do you travel far, or is it just a short
flight?

I guess life is rather like a ride in an
aeroplane.
How long it will last, we're not quite sure
or how long we will remain.

As when we set foot upon the plane, how
long it will take we do not know.
For if we have a delay it may take longer
to get to and fro.

Life too, is like this, how long it will last
of this we're unsure.
But we can remember life is eternal, who
could ask for more?

❋ ❋ ❋ ❋

What Lays Beyond the Moon?

Last night I stood and looked up at the
dark night sky.
There I saw half the moon shining way
up high.

As I gazed at it, I realised I was looking
no further than that.
Then the question came to mind - what
lays beyond the Moon, no one has the
facts?

My mind began to wonder and I thought
what might be there.
Perhaps somewhere free and open, where
our spirits will have their care.

Where the rays of the Sun, by day, will
warm us.
And gentle moonlight, by night, will
soothe and calm us.

So could the Moon, hung up high in
the sky.
Be a welcoming beacon for you and I?

To perhaps, one day, greet us all.
For when the time comes when we hear
our call?

❋ ❋ ❋ ❋

Heaven Is In Your Hand

Heaven is a wonderful place,
Where everyone has a happy face.
Where problems flee and are no more,
A place you must try to picture before.

It's somewhere that we all need to face.
We should all think of it, just in case!
No need to worry, nothing to fear.
As no one there sheds a tear.

There is no pain, no suffering there.
Once more I say, "There is nothing to
fear."
And although you'll be there and not
here.
We must always remember the spirit is
near.

Now please feel better if you can,
Knowing heaven is in your hand.
So one day when you are called, don't
cry "Oh no!"
But instead, with peace, say, "Let me
go. . . ."

❈ ❈ ❈ ❈

Beyond The Sun

From me you have been taken away.
By my side, of course, I should have
loved you to stay.

Even though you are no longer here,
your presence is all about me.
I know you're near, you are as always,
there's nothing to fear.

For we two are one, and this can't be
undone.
One day we will be together beyond the
Sun.

I know you'll be there to welcome me.
Standing before me, wonderful to see,
arms outstretched, you will be my key.

So this I know, it's not the end, but a
beginning of something lovely.
Now my heart again is singing, so it
could be said, this is a new beginning.

❋ ❋ ❋ ❋

Only a Breath Away

There is nothing for you to worry
about or fear.
Because you should know that
your lost one is near.
With all their thoughts and
feelings you hold dear.

Don't worry, they know you will
never forget.
You must know they don't want
you to be upset.
They know you have done nothing
to regret.

So gain comfort from all of this in
your mind.
And their understanding and love
you will always find.
As they are only a breath away,
remember this always for all of
your days.

❋ ❋ ❋ ❋

The Pathway of Your Future

May you both feel about you,
happiness, love and light.
As now the pathway of your future
is clearly set in sight.

Be guided by those about you,
have in them and in yourselves,
faith and trust.
Follow your hearts, love and care
for all about you, this I think, you
know you must.

For you have a wonderful time in
front of you both.
Which will last long after you
pledge your troth.

So love, peace and light surround
the two of you.
In all that you say and all that you
do.

❋ ❋ ❋ ❋

We'll Get Through . . .
Me and You

There is so much we have to
   do.
If we are to see our lives right
   through.

We have many hurdles to
   overcome.
We have many difficult tasks
   which have to be done.

We have so many lessons to
   learn.
So many pleasures to have,
   when it's our turn.

There are many, many things
   to do.
But I know, together we'll get
   through. . . .me and you!

❊ ❊ ❊ ❊

Bundle of Love

Dear little child, who was from
   heaven sent.
Unto those for whom you were
   truly meant.

Who has brought such joy to so
   many.
To those who thought there
   wouldn't be any.

A child who is indeed a gift from
   above.
Who has brought with him
   bundles full of love.

❈ ❈ ❈ ❈

Children at Heart

Are you still a child at heart?
Raring to go and make a start.

Are you still a child at heart?
Still excited at the arrival of your
birthday card.

Are you still a child at heart?
Very often wanting to put 'the
horse before the cart'.

Are you still a child at heart?
You feel entitled to the last jam
tart.

Are you still a child at heart?
And still like to be tucked in
when it gets dark.

Are you still a child at heart?
Life still has it's difficult parts.

Are you still a child at heart?
Of course you are - all of us are
children at heart!

❋ ❋ ❋ ❋

How Many People?

Do you stop to consider how many people
you know?
How many you have met in the past, and
how many there are as yet you do not know?

I bet if you counted, there would be a lot
more than you would think.
And if you could foresee the others you will
meet, it would really make you blink!

Now, think carefully to yourself - how do
people see you?
Why not stand back and look at yourself
with a detached view.

Well, what do you see, is it someone
cheerful, caring, loving and sincere?
Or do you see someone who you'd rather
not - and if you saw them coming you'd
say "Oh dear!"

Well remember no matter what you find,
that each of us drop like pebbles into a
pool, and our ripples go further out.
And each and everyone you meet, will be
aware of the sort of ripples you give out.

❉ ❉ ❉ ❉

The Patchwork of Life

All things in life are like a patchwork
quilt - they are all joined together.
People, animals, nature and even the
weather.

Each piece has a glorious pattern to
compliment the other.
Rather like a sister and brother or
father and mother.

Every person has something about
them that is so different from the next.
They have personalities and talents,
sometimes hidden, we didn't expect.

But each piece of the patchwork fits so
beautifully with the rest.
And each of the pieces that surround
us are the ones that match the best.

Further beyond this contrasting pieces
are being added on.
Which enrich and enhance life's patch-
work of which we can grow so fond.

❀ ❀ ❀ ❀

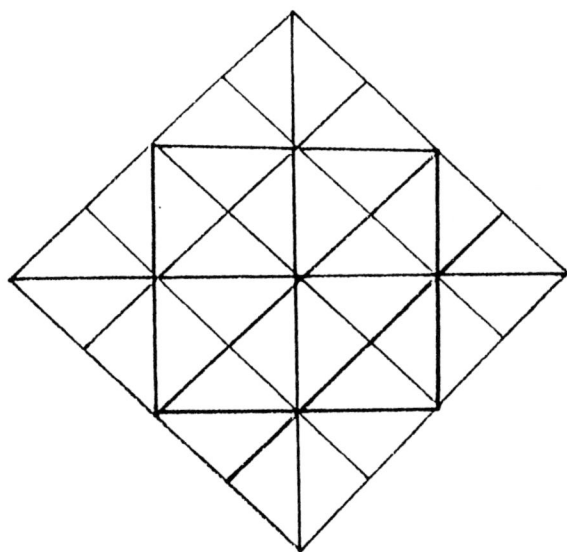

First Impressions

Do not judge before you know,
For what you think may not be
so.

Watch a while before you decide
Whether it be right, or is there
another side?

Because things are not always
what they first seem.
Like the difference between reality
or a dream.

So try not to draw conclusions as
you go along.
Remember, first impressions can
very easily be wrong.

❊ ❊ ❊ ❊

Who?

Have you ever talked with someone
on a bus or train?
Or had a little chat in the pouring
rain?

And found you enjoyed it, talking of
this and that.
But you don't know who it was to
whom you chatted, whilst you sat.

Have you ever done this and never
asked their name?
And then thought, long after,
wasn't it a shame.

But fate throws these meetings
along our way.
So we might wander home and say
"What a lovely person! What a lovely
day!"

✻ ✻ ✻ ✻

Use The Correct Key

People are like keys, they don't
always fit.
Sometimes you have to wiggle
them a bit!

Then the key slots in the lock.
Which sometimes comes as a bit
of a shock.

The door then swings open wide.
So you can then step inside.

Remember people are rather like
your keys.
And when they unlock they open
up with ease.

So don't be frustrated if you at
first can't step within.
Be patient, eventually the correct
key will enable you to wander in.

❋ ❋ ❋ ❋

Person Within

Do not judge people purely by
what you see.
Have a chat with them and let the
speech flow free.

As when you allow the words to
come tumbling out.
You learn what's held within -
what they think about.

Sometimes a simple chat just at
the right time.
Enables you to really know
someone, as you're allowed within
a space we all call mine.

For it is here the true person lives
- not the one you see.
But the person within that likes to
be set free!

❋ ❋ ❋ ❋

Dip Your Toe in the Water

Don't judge others by what they
say or how they look.
As sometimes we can be wrong
and are mistook.

Don't 'tar everyone with the
same brush'.
Don't be quick to draw
conclusions, there's no rush!

Would you jump into a pool -
just like that?
Or would you dip your toe in
before you go splat?

As to jump into the pool when
the temperature you hadn't
tried.
You would end up experiencing
a nasty surprise.

So tread gently into a
friendship, stick your toe in
first and try.
Then if you don't find the water
too warm you'll have time to
think, Why?

But always remember - learn
about others for yourself in
your own way.
You can listen to but not
always believe what others say.

You will, of course, be rewarded
with friendship of great worth.
Which will last through
eternity, in Heaven and on
Earth.

❉ ❉ ❉ ❉

Friendly Blessings

Thank you Lord for my dear
friends.
Who give me love without end.

Thank you for their kindly way.
Which helps me through day by
day.

Thank you for their ear they
lend.
Which like this my troubles they
help mend.

Thank you for their shoulder on
which I cry.
On which I know I can rely.

Thank you for the time they give.
Which in turn helps it easier to
live.

Send them Lord, blessing
without end.
To all of them, my ever faithful
friends.

❄ ❄ ❄ ❄

Friends from Afar

When people visit from far away.
Don't let shyness stand in the
way.

You don't know what to say?
But be sure, they feel the same
way.

It's really a relief, you'd never
believe.
You know, they're just like you
and me!

We dress the same, nearly think
the same.
And just like us they hate the
rain!

So now it's time for you to go.
We wish you well, we hope you
know?

We enjoyed your visit, your
company too.
And look forward again, to
saying "How are you?"

* * * *

Friendship Knack

Sometimes it's funny how life
can be.
Sometimes good for you and
not for me.
Then suddenly the tables turn.
Then it's time for you to yearn.

But if we two can good friends
be.
Things will be just fine for you
and me.
We will each have a shoulder to
cry on.
A really good friend we know we
can rely on.

Because having a friend close
by your side.
The rubble of life can no further
slide.
The firm hand of friendship can
hold it all back.
And you and I have that
Friendship Knack!

* * * *

My Very Best Friend

I know you are at home waiting
   for me.
So eager for your face, I am to
   see.

We've only been apart . . . one
   day.
But already there's so much to
   say.

Like I miss you, I love you, I
   hate being apart.
It's like being all alone in the
   dark.

But soon I'll be home, we'll be
   together again.
My husband, my lover, my very
   best friend.

❄ ❄ ❄ ❄

Not Just Me

Your love surrounds me day by
day.
When I feel I'm aware then there is
always a way.

When things feel awkward and
difficult, as sometimes they do.
I know it's not just me to cope on
my own, I know there's you.

You lighten my load, warm my
heart, cleanse my mind.
And with your help, eventually
the answer I find.

❋ ❋ ❋ ❋

The Helper

I can't imagine life without you.
You have been around for so long.
You have guided me and comforted me,
Whether I do right or wrong.

You strengthen my heart and mind,
So they both may feel protected.
You help me sort out my cares and
worries,
So that in the end some are rejected.

You unburden me, listen to my heart,
And enable me to feel light.
You surround me, uphold me,
In the never ending light.

❋ ❋ ❋ ❋

A Supporting Role

Do you look after all those you
hold dear, do they know you care?
Do they know you are there to
help and to listen, and with you
their troubles they can share?

Do they know that you think of
them and love them, from deep
within your heart?
Do you play to the full, your
most important part?

That is a supporting role that
keeps everything on an even keel.
But most of all those who you hold
dear, must know how you feel.

❄ ❄ ❄ ❄

Thank You Mum and Dad

We really have a wonderful
    Mum and Dad.
Their love and support we've
    always had.

Always there for your trouble
    to share.
They never ignore, they always
    care.

We love, we laugh, rarely shed
    a tear.
We feel we can say or ask,
    without nothing to fear.

They always have so much
    time to give.
Thanks to them, we happily
    live.

They're always there at your
    side,
Your soothing, ever loving
    guide.

So thank you to our wonderful
    Dad and Mum,
For all the many things you've
    done.

But most of all what we must
    do,
Is thank you, Mum and Dad
    for being you.

✳ ✳ ✳ ✳

'Man's Best Friend'

You were our very loyal friend.
Who protected and served us to
your end.

You were always there to greet
us home.
Eyes bright, tale wagging, to
almost everyone!

We miss you now, we always
will.
The house feels quiet, empty
and still.

But our fond memories of you
are still there.
Somehow I know that you watch
over us and care.

❀ ❀ ❀ ❀

Mr. Snail

Oh! little snail how you struggle with
your house upon your back.
You must always feel you're climbing
up hill, even though you're only on the
flat.

You meander along to pastures new.
Where you hope to find for you,
troubles are few.

Oh! Mr. Snail, we like you sometimes
feel life is an uphill struggle.
Suddenly, we too are in a bit of a
muddle.

But I guess we should take a tip from
you, to gain some light relief.
And do as you do, when the time is
right, and turn over a new leaf.

❄ ❄ ❄ ❄

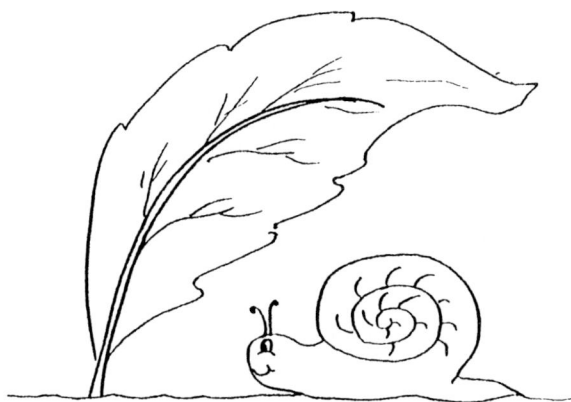

Good Morning Cobwebs!

Have you ever noticed how
cobwebs appear over night?
You find them first thing in the
morning, covered in dew, such
a pretty sight!

You find this item of nature's
work of art, sometimes in a tree
or hedge.
Not knowing where the spider
made it's start.

It shimmers and twinkles in the
light morning breeze.
It shines in the Sun this
complex pattern, engineered
with such skill and ease.

❋ ❋ ❋ ❋

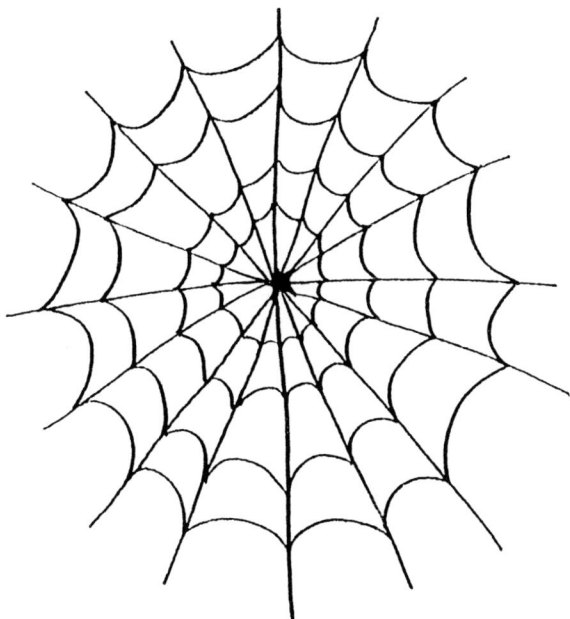

Rainbow, Rainbow

Rainbow, rainbow, way up high,
Your beautiful colours delight the
eye.

For these wonderful shades form
a glorious arch,
Which appear never to end, or
even start.

Rainbow, rainbow, you always
appear when we need you most.
When dark skies are looming, you
arrive almost like a heavenly host.

❋ ❋ ❋ ❋

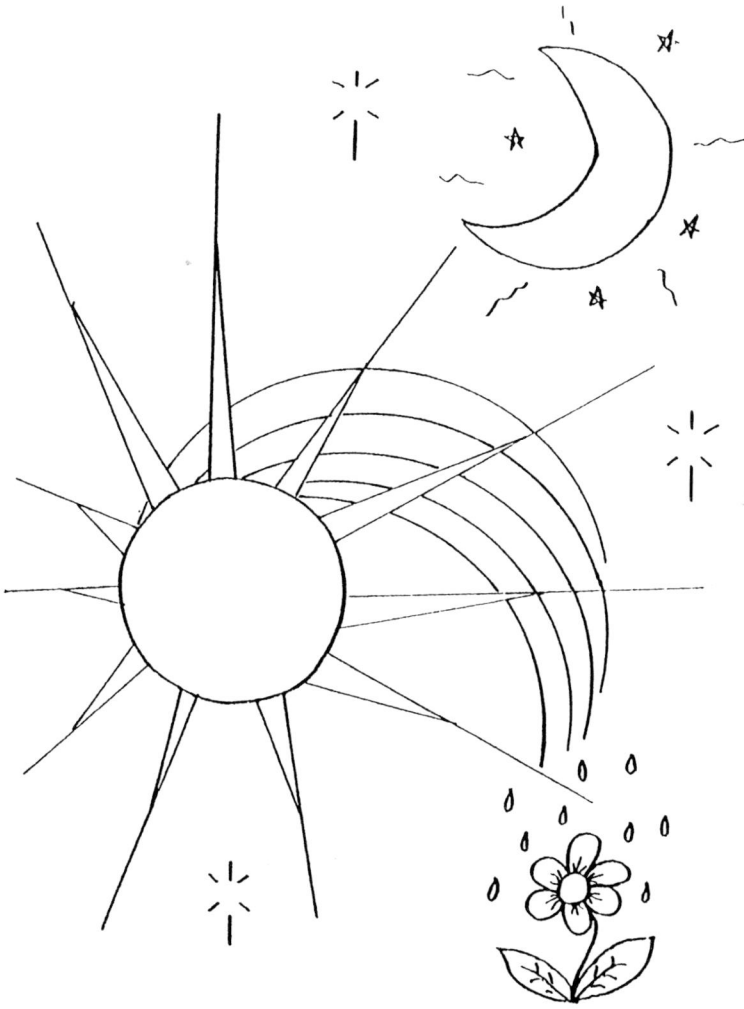

Like Mud in the Pouring Rain

Let all go on about you wherever
you may be.
Let mundane things wash about
you and let your mind wander free.

So if you have jobs before you, and
they're the ones you dread.
Go about them and let your mind
drift, keep your eyes ahead.

Because the things that trouble you
are often trivial and mundane.
So let them be washed away, like
mud in the pouring rain.

❄ ❄ ❄ ❄

The Rain Shouldn't be Forsaken

Today we had a shower of rain,
And somehow it washed away the
strain.

As when it stopped, I stepped outside,
And I felt all my cares and worries
subside.

Everywhere was refreshed, more
beautiful and bright.
Leaves and grass were glistening, such
a pretty sight.

Inside I too felt as if I were glistening.
And stood refreshed as I was listening.

The birds sang cheerfully a sweet sound
so clear.
They too had that feeling we should all
hold dear.

That is, when it rains we could all feel
awakened.
So don't be angry when it rains, for it
shouldn't be forsaken.

❅ ❅ ❅ ❅

Sparkling Layer

Oh gentle rain - as mist
   does fall.
On varied leaves that
   cover all.

Little droplets sparkle like
   nature's diamonds.
Shining bright, like glazed
   almonds!

The leaves shimmer with
   their wet look.
For green glass, they
   could be mistook.

For the rain changes the
   picture as it falls.
As a gentle sparkling layer
   covers all.

❈ ❈ ❈ ❈

Water, Water Everywhere

Water all about us seeps,
Further and further it creeps.

Trickling on and on each and
every day.
Where does it start? Well we
really can't say.

It passes us by as rivers or
streams.
And even is included, in the
odd dream.

Water is about us everywhere.
And wherever it may be, people
stop and stare.

For water is not only pleasing
to the eye.
It cleanses us and cheers us, as
it passes by.

❇ ❇ ❇ ❇

Life Is Like a Pond

Life is like a pond, when you
really look into it, there is a
great deal to see.
There is so much hiding within,
for you and me.

If you peer right to the very
bottom, you can't believe
your eyes.
Pebbles and gravel swishing
gently this way and that, then
quietly again it lies.

Underwater plant life sway
like corn in a breeze.
And glimmers and shimmers
for your eyes to please.

Life also has hidden within,
beauties so often left untold.
But like the pond, sometimes
you have to peer deeper within,
then like a flower it will unfold.

❋ ❋ ❋ ❋

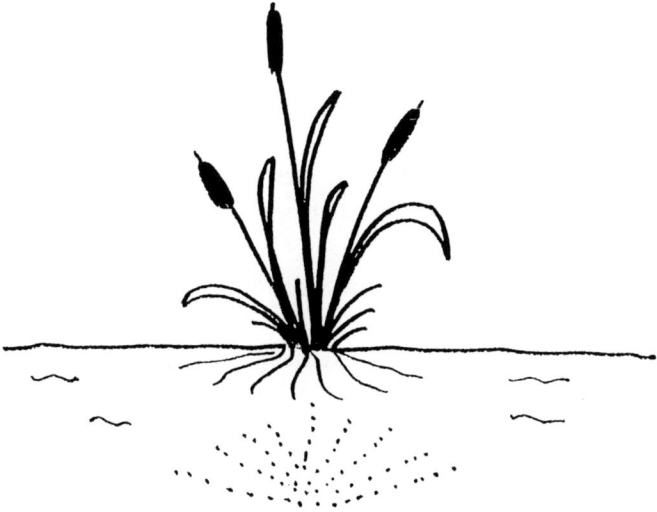

Water In Your Mind

Can you imagine water in your
mind?
Cleansing it, refreshing it, feeling
cool and kind.

Trickling gently, seeping here and
there.
Washing away the trivial and
leaving only what needs most care.

This, from time to time, we should
all try to do.
Then our minds would feel relaxed
and calm, we could count our
blessings and see our troubles are
few.

✻ ✻ ✻ ✻

Noah's Rainbow

Today I saw a rainbow just above
the sea.
A place where I'd never seen one
before, could it really be?

Such a lovely arch of colours, so
vivid and so clear.
Quite a beautiful spectacle to see,
a moment to hold dear.

Could that have been the same
rainbow Noah was so glad to
behold?
That was his sign from God of
which the Bible told.

So remember when you next gaze
at a rainbow, it could be that very
one.
Think of and thank Noah, for the
wonders that were done.

❈ ❈ ❈ ❈

Seaside Paddle

Is the tide going out or coming in,
I'm never quite sure?
I guess I must stand here and
watch the waves a little more.

Gently a wave comes and laps my
feet.
Then further in between my toes,
the sand does seep.

You can taste the salt in the
breeze.
And the soothing whoosh of the
tide helps me feel at ease.

Gradually, as time goes by,
The waves withdraw as seagulls
cry.

Refreshed I turn my back and
walk away.
But know for sure I'll be back one
day.

❉ ❉ ❉ ❉

Unseen Like the Wind

Have you ever watched a
windmill when it's going
round?
The wind seems to come from
one direction - is that what you
have found?

Then it stops, and suddenly the
blades turn the opposite way.
And the corn in the field, it too
sways the same way.

This is simply achieved by the
force of the wind alone.
Unseen, unheard, so graceful,
no engines to groan.

There's not only the wind but
there are other forces you
cannot see.
Do not underestimate them,
as they can do so much for you
and me.

The power of love, thought and
prayer.
These like the wind you cannot
see, but are truly there.

These forces can affect the
windmills of our souls, hearts
and minds.
They can whirl us around,
then eventually peace and
tranquillity we will really find.

❀ ❀ ❀ ❀

The Wind of Change

The wind of change occasionally
blows through our lives.
Along with it's changes it leaves
debris, these are our strifes.

For sometimes the wind of change
blows our lives around.
Blowing so hard, it turns our world
upside down.

Suddenly nothing seems the same
any more.
And all you would like is that all
could be as it was before

It is at times like these we should
remember, eventually all winds die
out.
So we can gain comfort that the
wind of change, it too will peter
out.

And leave behind it a feeling of
relief and calm.
And after this we'll see, on
reflection, to us it did not harm.

❋ ❋ ❋ ❋

There Dawns a Fresh Start

Spring is coming, it's on it's
way.
We now have more light day
by day.

Trees are budding with new
life not yet seen.
And bulbs are shooting so early
it seems.

Snowdrops have graced us
with a freshness.
And in winter months have
granted us gladness.

We look forward with this
gladness in our hearts.
As Spring approaches and
soon makes it's start.

We yearn for the arrival of
some of our favourite flowers.
Daffodils and crocuses, yellow
and lilac - just two of the
colours with therapeutic
powers.

For the colours of Spring lift
and gladden our hearts.
And encourages us to look
within and there dawns a fresh
start.

❈ ❈ ❈ ❈

It's Time for Spring

To the snowdrops we say
a fond farewell.
Spring is now coming, it's
time we can tell.

The gloom of Winter is
slipping slowly away.
More sunlight we have,
day by day.

Daffodils and crocuses are
bursting everywhere,
Lovely splashes of colour
at which we stop and
stare.

Showers of rain refresh
the blades of grass.
Restoring their emerald
colour, which none can
surpass.

Trees and hedges are
budding everywhere.
Birds are flying back and
forth, building their nests
with such care.

The sky is blue, the dark
grey colour has long gone.
There are white fluffy
clouds and the sweet birds
song.

So Spring is here, be glad
in it!
A beautiful time of
awakening - you have to
admit.

❀ ❀ ❀ ❀

Just Like . . .

Like a flower we unfold
hour by hour.

Like the singing of a bird
we too like it can be
heard.

Like the buzzing of a bee
we can hover free.

Like a yacht with strong
wind in its sail.
Like it, we move like a
flag in a gale.

Like bright sunshine
everywhere, we radiate
light which we can share.

From all this we learn,
all things are one.
Is that what the Lord
meant 'Thy will be done'?

❀ ❀ ❀ ❀

Easter Thoughts

Easter is an uplifting time to cheer
and strengthen all.
For we know Christ died for us, as
on our knees we fall.

We pray to give our thanks to you
for the risen Son.
Who guides, protects and upholds
each and everyone.

So when you wake on Easter
morn,
Be sure to thank the Lord that
Christ again is born.

Easter reminds us that God is ever
near.
So hold this thought to your heart,
and keep it ever dear.

❀ ❀ ❀ ❀

Nature's Confetti

The cherry blossom flutters in the
gentle breeze.
Floating down, dancing in the air
as it falls from the trees.

It's scattered all about, covering
the ground.
Just as confetti, after a wedding
can be found.

To me this cherry blossom is
nature's confetti so glorious to see.
For it signifies a special event,
when Spring says to Summer "Will
you marry me?"

❋ ❋ ❋ ❋

The Merry Month of May

Here it is - 'The merry month of May'.
During which it is my own birthday.

Here it is once again, so soon!
And the bluebells as usual, are in full
bloom.

It doesn't seem a year ago, since my
last Birthday.
"Now I'm a year older and wiser" - well,
so they say!

But I feel no different, I certainly don't
feel older!
I maybe feel more confident, perhaps a
little bolder!

Life shouldn't be measured in years,
But by joys, happiness and the odd few
tears.

For these are the riches which each of
our lives bring.
We should try to remember this when
"Happy Birthday" we sing.

❀ ❀ ❀ ❀

Garden Whispers

When I walk in my garden, there's
a buzzing all about me.
A sort of chattering from flower,
plant, bird and bee.

You can't quite hear what the
whispers are all about, indeed
what they're saying.
But my guess is, for warmth, love
and kindness, for this they are
praying.

So do not underestimate the
nature of life around you, but
show them the love and care for
which they ask.
And in return they will give their
thanks to you, which forever will
last.

❄ ❄ ❄ ❄

Don't Pave Out Your Garden

Do you have a garden and you've
thought 'I'll pave it out!'?
Because you're fed up with the
work that you could do without.

But then, after you've given it
some thought, you have a change
of heart.
You realise you would miss the
beauty of your garden - it would
leave a gap in your heart.

Life can also be hard work, rather
like your garden.
It has it's joys, but also has it's
burdens.

But we must never pave our lives,
blanking everything out.
Even though it's so easy just to
shut ourselves away, of this there
is no doubt.

But if we paved our lives, covering
all that is around.
We would not see the beauty, and
all the good there is also to be
found.

So tend life's garden, share it with
others as much as you can.
And even though it is sometimes
hard work, don't pave out your
fellow man.

* * * *

Appreciate Your Garden

Do you ever sit in your garden all
alone?
Just to appreciate that it is your
very own?

To remember it's a little piece of
countryside that will be left
unchanged.
A piece you can keep as you like,
and know it won't be rearranged.

Try not to take for granted this
very important fact.
Bring those to mind who have no
garden, think of them whilst
you're sat.

If you have a garden, remember
how lucky you are.
Be grateful, and thank your lucky
stars.

❀ ❀ ❀ ❀

To Be Like a Rose

Oh! gentle rose, waving in the
breeze, swaying from side to side.
Hold your petals tight, don't let
them fall, stand firm with dignity
and pride.

We, like the rose, must sometimes
hold ourselves together.
As sometimes in life we, like it,
experience a type of turbulent
weather.

We feel pulled this way and that,
rather like the rose.
We don't know which way to turn,
or how we'll cope no one knows.

But when you next walk into
turbulent weather,
Why not remember the rose, and
like it try and hold yourself
together.

❋ ❋ ❋ ❋

Brambles of Your Mind

Have you ever come across a bramble
in your garden,
And no matter what you do, it prickles
and it tangles round and it clings on to
you?

No matter how you try, it persists,
prickling and piercing your skin.
And eventually, after struggling, you
cut yourself free and place the bramble
in the bin.

We too must do this with the brambles
of our minds.
We must cut ourselves free of trouble
and get rid of what we find.

For if we do not cut the brambles from
our minds.
We are just allowing the troubling
offender to become more intertwined.

So root them out, send them off, clear
them from your thoughts.
By doing this you let more joy in, so
pull out the brambles, you know you
really ought!

❊ ❊ ❊ ❊

The Rose of Life

Our life is like a rose, growing
good and strong.
We, like it, have our roots - a
feeling of where we belong.

We have a stem running through
our lives.
And we too, have thorns - these
are our strifes.

But will the rose flower, this no
one knows?
That is up to the person for which
it grows.

But if watered and cared for, we
shall be blessed with a bloom.
So if we too wish to be blessed in
the same way, we must tend our
rose very soon.

❀ ❀ ❀ ❀

Cutting The Hedge

Today we cut our garden hedge.
And when we finished it we made
a pledge.

Next time we won't let it get so long.
We should cut it more often, that's
where we go wrong!

Our thoughts and beliefs are a bit like
the hedge.
They too, need trimming and shaping
before we become misled.

We need to tidy our minds, cutting out
our old thoughts, which are, in a sense,
dead.
Just as we do whilst cutting and
shaping our garden hedge.

And as when the hedge is tidy and
complete.
Our thoughts are the same - we really
have achieved a wonderful feat.

❄ ❄ ❄ ❄

Growing Like a Lawn

Have you ever thought of yourself
as a garden lawn?
Oh dear! how boring you think, and
then you start to yawn.

But when you consider a lawn with
a little more thought.
Much is given from it and from it we
could be taught.

A lawn is forever growing and needs
to be kept in trim.
Rather like our minds and bodies,
it's just a case of where to begin!

If you care for your lawn, trim it,
feed it and weed it, it will bring you
much pleasure.
Care for yourself in a similar way
and your life will become a pleasure.

✳ ✳ ✳ ✳

A Promise of What Is To Come

Heavenly Father you have given to
us, amongst many, the gift of trees.
So many shapes and sizes so
beautiful to see.

They grace us in the Spring with
fresh bright colours of green.
And in the Autumn, glorious warm
colours, nowhere else they can be
seen.

In the Winter most stand bare,
silhouetted against the Winter sky.
But holding within a promise deep
inside.

All year round trees are a promise
of what is to come.
"Our Father in Heaven, Thy will be
done."

✳ ✳ ✳ ✳

The Sunset

Gently the Sun sets, almost as if
resting on the silhouette of the
skyline.
Orange, yellow, pink, white, red
and blue intermingle to produce a
picture so fine.

So peaceful but uplifting, calming
and soothing to the eye.
This beautiful, glorious collage
which besets the evening sky.

Very gently it slowly and magically
all slips away.
Now to be kept from our sight until
another day.

✻ ✻ ✻ ✻

Angelic Stars

When I step into the dark, what do I see?
When I look up, I see the bright starts
twinkling back at me.

There they dangle so far up high.
Lighting up the dark night sky.

What are these stars that are way off
yonder?
This is a thought on which I ponder.

Well, my guess is that God created stars,
To remind us of angelic hosts from afar.

For I believe to each star in the sky,
There is held within, angelic love which
can fly.

It darts here and there, showering us all.
Dusting us lightly before the cockerel's
call.

Then safely it is whisked away.
And we eagerly await another visit again
at the end of the day.

❀ ❀ ❀ ❀

Forty Shades of Green

There is an old Somerset saying, "There
are forty shades of green."
And from my kitchen window, I'm sure all
forty can be seen.

From the brightest shade of the beech
leaves so refreshing.
To the dark glossy holly, that reminds us
of the Christmas blessing.

Fields and hedges appear to overlap one
another.
All of them green, but each not like the
other!

So when you have time to look out of your
window and stare.
Try to count the forty shades, for they
must be there.

But if like me, this you try to do.
My guess is, you won't reach twenty-two!

As when you count, you look at the view
with a searching eye.
And the beauty will overtake you, leaving
you asking "Where was I?"

❋ ❋ ❋ ❋

The Power of Flowers

Never underestimate the energy
     in flowers.
For they not only possess beauty,
     but are blessed with powers.

They can calm and uplift you,
     guide and heal you too.
But unfortunately, those who
     realise, are all too few.

So why not ask the power of the
     flowers for their help?
And let them heal you, until you
     forget how you felt.

❋ ❋ ❋ ❋

The Organ Calls from the Church

On a glorious summers afternoon, I can
hear the organ's merry tune.
It calls out joyfully from the church
'please come soon'.

Beautiful skies of blue have light, white,
fluffy clouds,
Which have now long since seen the
morning dew.

Bumble bees busily work, whizzing from
flower to flower.
Birds sing sweetly and brighten further
this happy hour.

The church tower watches over us all,
keeping a gentle eye.
To see us safely through our lives - so give
a gentle sigh.

It is there for us all to share.
And for us it will always be there to care.

So play the organ loudly and bright.
That it may bring attention to our church,
and hold it within everyone's sight.

❈ ❈ ❈ ❈

Autumn-time Blessings

Summertime draws to a close.
Autumn winds begin to blow.

Leaves change to crimson gold.
Gently they crinkle and begin to
fold.

It is at this time, our Harvest
Thanksgiving.
A time to be grateful for the
countryside we live in.

For we have the sun, wind and
rain.
To help produce vegetables, fruit
and grain.

So don't be sad that Summer
draws to an end.
As Autumn-time holds blessings
without end.

❊ ❊ ❊ ❊

Bountiful Harvest

Autumn fast approaches, bringing
colours golden, brown and bright.
We have at this time our Harvest
Thanksgiving, such a glorious
sight.

Collections of fruit and vegetables
beautifully displayed.
Think if this was not so, how we
would feel dismayed.

For some are not so blessed as we
so fortunately are.
Try and spare a thought for them,
though they may be afar.

But of course remember this is
Harvest time, rejoice and be glad
in it.
Give thanks for such a bountiful
supply, to keep us fed and fit!

❋ ❋ ❋ ❋

Harvest Home

Bless us Lord, at this our Harvest
time.
Thank you for the world I call mine.

The sheep and cattle in the field
grazing.
The beauty of the countryside so
amazing.

Thank you for those who work the
land.
Who provide the food we have in our
hand.

There is much work we do not see.
Which takes place to provide food for
you and me.

Lord, how grateful I am for the land.
The hills, the valleys, the streams,
for the soil on which I stand.

The Sun, Moon and stars, wind and
the rain.
Which in turn, enables me to thank
you once again.

❋ ❋ ❋ ❋

Spring Song

Leaves of bronze and gold have
    fallen, all around they lie.
Leaving spindly trees silhouetted
    against the cold grey sky.

Frosty grass twinkling white,
    crunches beneath our feet.
This is the time Autumn says to
    Winter, "We must meet."

Now we can say that Winter is
    truly here.
As Christmas time draws ever
    near.

But never mind, the Winter won't
    be here for long.
Before we know, the birds will be
    singing their Spring song.

So when the dark Winter days
    linger on.
Why not sing in your heart, your
    own Spring song.

❋ ❋ ❋ ❋

A Church Along the Street

The shops are full of people
milling.
Looking for things for stocking
fillings.

Window displays of gifts and
decorations.
Each one made by people of
different nations.

Visit Santa in his grotto.
"Merry Christmas!" is his motto.

Amongst all of this stands a
church along the street.
Why not go in, and just take a
seat?

By just sitting in 'The House of
the Saviour'.
Think of this as doing yourself a
favour.

As when at the altar cross you
stare.
Admit the true meaning of
Christmas, go on, be fair.

And when you leave and close
the door.
You'll probably wish that you
visited before.

Because unlike the festive
windows at which we stare.
The altar cross will always be
there.

❃ ❃ ❃ ❃

The Christmas Eve Tree

On Christmas Eve churches hold
services of celebration at midnight.
Many gather together, pews will be
full, what a wonderful sight.

The uplifting sound of the beautiful
bells ringing.
The building will be full of strong
voices joyfully singing.

There will be a Christmas tree
standing there.
And if you can, take time out for at
it to stare.

For many years ago a tree like
that, stood in an important place.
It was beside the stable door,
where the babe was born, the tree
could see His face.

The tree was there, a lovely sight
to behold.
On that very night so bright and
cold.

So when at the tree you stare,
pretend you are there.
Although that babe is here and
now - for all of us He cares!

If to church you are unable to go,
perhaps you can't trudge through
the snow?
Gaze at your own tree, let it be a
gentle reminder.
Then His presence you will know.

❄ ❄ ❄ ❄

Hark! Is that Sleigh Bells?

The night sky is black, almost like
velvet, the stars are twinkling bright.
Hark! Is that sleigh bells I hear
ringing? it can't be there's no one in
sight.

Empty stockings hang around the
fireplace, will they be filled?
Little folk lay sleeping, waiting for
the morning, hoping to be thrilled.

The Moon is looking down, shining
upon the snow, crisp and white.
It's just right for Santa, surely he'll
visit tonight.

His sherry and mince pies await him
by the chimney corner, cosy and
warm.
He deserves his rewards, a little rest,
peace and calm!

Thank you Santa, for coming and
leaving presents under our tree.
"A very Merry Christmas, Santa, and
lots of love to you from me!"

❅ ❅ ❅ ❅

Festive Cheer

Isn't it strange how festive cheer
    can wipe away all our fear?
So why don't we keep festive
    cheer all year?

Why not keep the warm glow in
    our heart?
That enters with Christmas, right
    from the start.

Why not keep the happiness
    within?
That wells up inside us and helps
    combat sin.

Try to remember, Christmas is not
    just two days of the year.
It can be yours every day, just be
    open and hear.

For Christmas Angels are always
    about.
Ready to guide us and push away
    our doubt.

✻ ✻ ✻ ✻

Occasionally Look Back

Go along life's track and
occasionally look back.
Be happy at what you see,
that's the knack!

If you look carefully you will
see.
That we all have happiness,
you and me.

So give thanks for your
memories and be glad.
That most are happy and few
are sad.

❈ ❈ ❈ ❈

Let your light so shine before men, that they may see your good works, and glorify your Father which is in heaven.

Matthew 5-16

❋ ❋ ❋ ❋

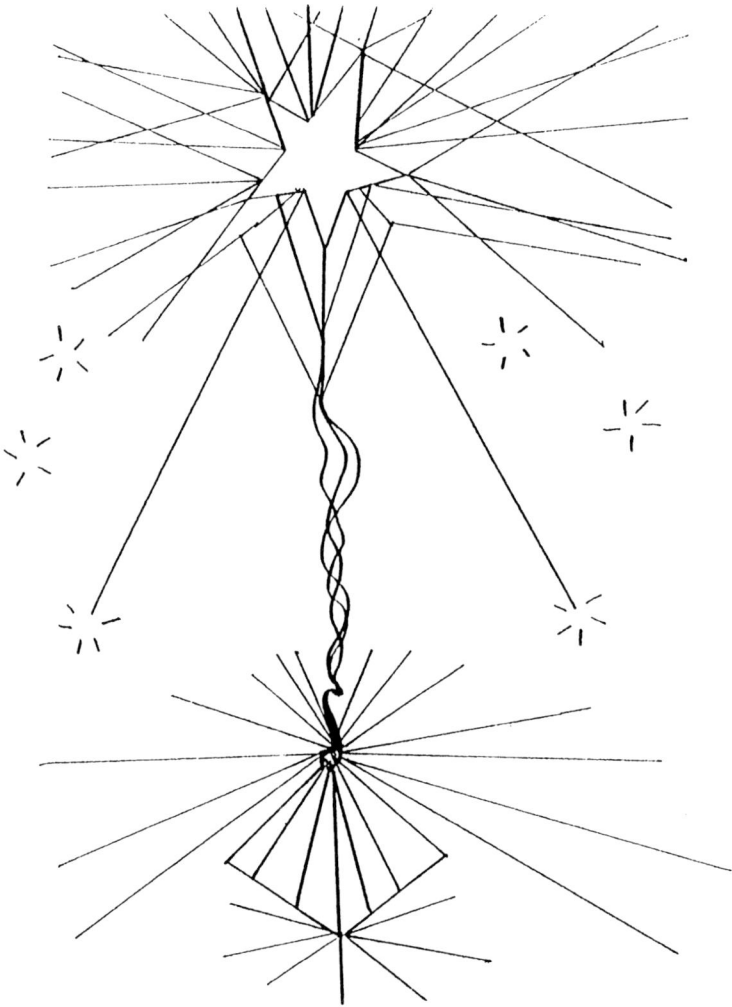

INDEX

ℰ ☙

℘ ℭ